NY GIANTS

SUPER BOWL XXV CHAMPS

BY DAN ABRAMSON

MODERN PUBLISHING
A DIVISION OF UNISYSTEMS, INC.
NEW YORK, NEW YORK 10022

CONTENTS

Jeff Hostetler—Super Bowl hero with the winning ball.
AP/Wide World Photos

INTRODUCTION

The Giants' locker room was a madhouse after Super Bowl XXV. Television cameras and newspaper reporters crowded together with ecstatic football players as the cheers of delighted fans echoed throughout Tampa Stadium long after the game ended.

Today, the Giants had triumphed over a very good Buffalo Bills team in one of the most exciting pro football games ever played—an event they had been working toward since their last Super Bowl win four years earlier, against the Denver Broncos!

Head coach, Bill Parcells and the team's owners watched as running back extraordinaire, Ottis Anderson, was presented with the Super Bowl Most Valuable Player award. Nobody could argue with the choice—Ottis had given everything he had for four grueling quarters lasting more than three hours. The Giants would not have won without him. Nor would they have won without quarterback-of-the-moment Jeff Hostetler, who had been filling in for the injured first-stringer, Phil Simms.

"Hoss," as his teammates call him, had been in winning clubhouses before, but only as a substitute player. Now *he* was the quarterback who had led the Giants to victory. A fact that would, undoubtedly, fuel the rivalry between these two players.

Although Hoss was soon due on stage to take a few bows of his own, who could doubt that he wasn't remembering—like a rerun of a favorite movie—the events that led up to this incredible Super Bowl victory. Especially, his own journey from second-stringer to starter to become a Super Bowl-winning quarterback...

Jeff Hostetler completed a pass in the NFC Championship game against the 49ers. *Thearon Henderson/Focus on Sports*

Master quarterback, Phil Simms was ready to hit his mark. *Focus on Sports*

1 HOSTETLER VS. SIMMS

When the Giants opened training camp in July 1990, quarterbacks Phil Simms and Jeff Hostetler were preparing for the season ahead. But Giants fans and reporters alike, were already wondering who would lead the team in the months ahead.

Both in the club and out, everyone knew that Hoss was an excellent quarterback, they also knew that Simms was an excellent quarterback with far more experience. Since only one of them could play, it seemed obvious that Simms—the first-stringer and starter—was going to get even more experience while Hoss—the second-stringer and backup—would remain on the sidelines.

Although every team needs backup and reserve players—just in case the first stringer is injured or otherwise—it's the nature of the game and the players to want to be the reigning football hero—Hostetler was no different. But ever since the 1979 college draft, Simms had been the Giants' first choice quarterback.

Simms and Hostetler were both 6 foot 3 inches and weighed approximately 210 pounds, but their quarterbacking styles were vastly different. Simms played the old-fashioned way. He was a classic "drop-back" passer, who fades back behind his blockers and waits to throw until a receiver is open. Quarterbacks like this sometimes get tackled, or "sacked," for big losses. But a good drop-back passer like Simms throws very few interceptions and almost never fumbles the ball away.

Hoss, on the other hand, was a "scrambler." He sometimes dropped back behind his blockers and sometimes ran away from them to confuse the defense. A scrambling quarterback can either run with the ball himself or throw downfield while he is running. But that is not easy to do. Many scramblers over the years have led the league in the number of interceptions and fumbles they have given up. Although Hoss was sure-handed, that statistic counted against him from the start.

Giants' coach Bill Parcells was a careful man, who believed that the winning team in most football games was the one that gave up the fewest interceptions and fumbles. From the beginning, Parcells regarded Simms as a sure thing and played him as often as possible. That proved dangerous for Simms, because the Giants did not have particularly good blocking in his first few seasons. A scrambling quarterback might have been able to dodge around tacklers better than Simms, who took a fearful beating. But gradually, the situation improved and Parcells who admired Simms' courage and ability, kept him on the front line.

But the Giants' first post-Super Bowl season ended in a losing record. The year after that, the Giants went 10–6 but failed to make the playoffs. Then, in 1989, they won their division and qualified for the playoffs, only to lose to Los Angeles in a badly played game that centered on an intercepted pass that Simms should never have thrown.

Through all of this, the stoic Jeff Hostetler stayed on the sidelines and watched.

In 1988 when Hoss finally did get to start a game, against New Orleans, he thought he did well in the first half. But Parcells told him that Jeff Rutledge was playing in the second half. Hoss was extremely angry and demanded to be traded, but the Giants refused. They told him he had too much potential and that they might need him if Simms and Rutledge got hurt.

Lawrence Taylor and Jeff Hostetler were psyched after Hoss handed off a touchdown. *AP/Wide World Photos*

So Hoss did the kind of things that reserve quarterbacks always do. He held the football for the placekicker on field goal attempts—which is much more difficult than it looks. He also kept the charts on each opposing team, writing down the sort of play they used in any given situation. The charts would then be put on the Giants' computer database, to be used when they played the same opponent the next time. Compared to the life Simms was living, that was all extremely dull for Hoss.

Then, in 1989, Hoss was promoted to number two quarterback and actually got to start twice when Simms was injured. The Giants won both games and Hoss threw a touchdown pass in each. He also showed some fancy footwork, running around tacklers—and sometimes leaping over them—to roaring cheers from the Giants' fans.

But Simms recovered and Parcells put him back in the game. Hostetler returned to the bench. It was one of Parcells' rules that you should never replace a player just because he got hurt, no matter how well the backup played. To do so would be unfair to the injured man.

Hoss' play in those two games did, however, convince the Giants that he was a solid second-string player. So they let go of Rutledge and replaced him with Matt Cavanaugh, who had been a backup for most of his 13 years in pro football. Parcells assured Hoss that he was still the second quarterback. Cavanaugh was there in case both Simms and Hoss got hurt.

So, as training camp opened in 1990, Hoss did thousands of pushups and situps and ran hundreds of laps around the training field. He attended meetings with the coaches and with Simms and Cavanaugh, where they discussed the various methods they might use against each team on their 1990 schedule. Hoss worked with the "B" team and watched, from across the field, as Simms worked with the first-stringers.

Officially, the team still had not yet decided whether Simms or Hostetler would be their starting quarterback. The suggestion that Hoss might be chosen was mainly to give the reporters something to write and talk about through the long summer weeks.

After his victory in Super Bowl XXI, Phil Simms appeared on "The Tonight Show" with guest-host Garry Shandling. *AP/Wide World Photos*

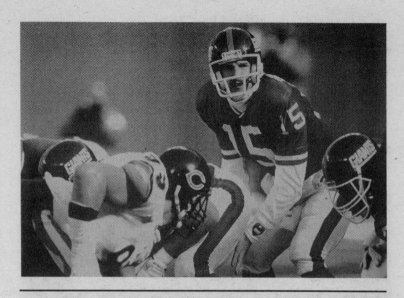

Jeff Hostetler took the snap against the Bears. *Focus on Sports*

LT attacked the quarterback in the Miami vs. New York game. *Focus on Sports*

2 THE TEAM ASSEMBLES

Of course, there is more to a pro football team than just the quarterback, although that is the most important position. Besides the three quarterbacks, there are 44 other guys on the team and several players show up at camp to compete for each of those 44 jobs.

For every rookie who makes the team, an older player has to be cut. This is one reason why training camps are so competitive.

Then again, there are some guys like Phil Simms and Jeff Hostetler who were good examples of players who knew they would be on the 1990 team, even though Hoss would probably be second-string.

There are three "platoons" on every team: offense, defense and the kicking squad. The kicking squad is usually made up of younger players trying to prove themselves.

The Giants' offense included five linesmen who played well the previous season: tackles, John Elliot and Doug Reisenberg; guards, Eric Moore and William Roberts; and center, Bart Oates.

They'd been playing as a unit for several years and each man knew how the others were likely to react in any given situation. From a distance, they looked like a group of elephants charging down the field. The shoulder pads and hip pads required by the league made these galloping giants look even more frightening—this line of offense had a combined weight of more than half a ton!

But you don't have to be huge to play pro football. One good example of that is Stephen Baker, who plays wide receiver and lines up next to those behemoths. Baker a.k.a., "The Touchdown Maker," is 5 feet 8 inches and weighs 160 pounds.

Other wide receivers were Mark Ingram and Odessa Turner. Wide receivers line up a "wide" distance away from the offensive line. Tight ends, who both catch passes and block defenders, get their name from the fact that they line up "tight" near the line. The Giants' Mark Bavaro was considered one of the best tight ends in football. At 6 feet 4 inches and 245 pounds, Bavaro was about average size for a tight end. When running full-speed he looked something like a small truck.

Then there were the running backs. Usually, each team plays one "blocking back," or fullback and one runner, or halfback, on each play. But that can be changed any time the coach wants. Maurice Carthon, the Giants' fullback, was one of the finest blockers in football. But after that, the squad fell apart. The Giants' first draft pick in 1990, Rodney Hampton, was a good runner who had no pro experience, and Coach Parcells didn't like to play rookies. Dave Meggett, smaller than Stephen Baker, was useful as a kick and punt returner, but Parcells didn't use him very often, either.

The most experienced running back in camp, Ottis Anderson, was considered an old man at 33. Anderson had been a superstar for the St. Louis Cardinals football team in the late 1970s and early 1980s. The Giants had traded for him as a reserve in their first Super Bowl year. When Ottis scored a touchdown for them in that Super Bowl, most fans thought it was a marvelous way for Anderson to finish his career. But he kept returning to the Giants' training camps in 1987–89 and had won a job each year. In 1990, he was back and confident as ever that he could still play pro football.

14

Mark Bavaro was the Giants' top possession receiver.
Focus on Sports

Ottis Anderson, the man who would not quit. *Focus on Sports*

On defense, the best Giants' linesman, Leonard Marshall, had not reported to camp because he wanted more money than the Giants were willing to pay. This did not worry the team much, because they had other good linesmen, such as Erik Howard, John Washington and Eric Dorsey. Only three linesmen play at a time and since a rookie named Mike Fox looked impressive, the general feeling was that Leonard Marshall was making a serious mistake.

Four men played downfield as defensive backs to guard the other team's pass receivers and the Giants were well-stocked at those positions. Mark Collins and Greg Jackson were the best of them. Myron Guyton, Adrian White and Perry Williams were also quite good. Just before the season, the Giants also signed Dave Duerson and Everson Walls. Both of them were getting older, but were still excellent players, and Coach Parcells always tried to sign as many experienced pros as he could find.

On their kicking team, Sean Landeta was a marvelous punter who boomed the football far down the field and way up in the air. Running back Dave Meggett was a superb return man who caused the opposition many sleepless nights. At 5 feet 7 inches and 180 pounds, Meggett was so small that he could lose himself among the bigger players on the field. People trying to tackle him had trouble seeing him. He could change directions at high speed, leaving would-be tacklers lying on the ground in despair.

The Giants' linebackers were Carl Banks, Pepper Johnson, Gary Reasons and Steve DeOssie.

But the finest team member of all, Lawrence Taylor—quite possibly the best linebacker ever—was not in camp. This was cause for serious worry.

He had been with the team for ten years, longer than anyone except Simms. Taylor combined awesome physical strength with the kind of speed you don't often find. He also had extraordinary intuition, which enabled him to guess in advance what the other team was about to do. To say that other quarterbacks feared Lawrence Taylor was putting it mildly. And he was always at his best in difficult situations.

"LT," as he liked to be called, was holding out for a higher salary than the Giants were paying him. As with Leonard Marshall, the team had pretended not to care, stating that they had plenty of other linebackers. No one was fooled. The other Giants' linebackers were excellent, but Taylor was in a league by himself.

As the summer went by, however, many Giants began to ask if Taylor realized how serious it was to miss the entire six weeks of training camp. Anyone could miss two weeks and still have a good season. A super player like LT might be able to skip four of the six weeks and still play well. But to miss all six weeks was dangerous. Conditioning is of great importance to an athlete facing a long season. The Giants would have to play 16 regular-scheduled games. Then, if all went well, they would play three post-season games, the last being the Super Bowl.

Most of the experts felt that the Giants—with Taylor —had a fine chance of getting to that championship game. Without LT, the feeling was that the Giants were just another half-decent team. The Giants themselves had doubts about getting to the Super Bowl without LT— or with LT if he was out of shape.

In the Giants training camp itself, all other concerns became secondary. The Giants knew that whoever was the starting quarterback, the job would be far more difficult on a team that did not include Lawrence Taylor.

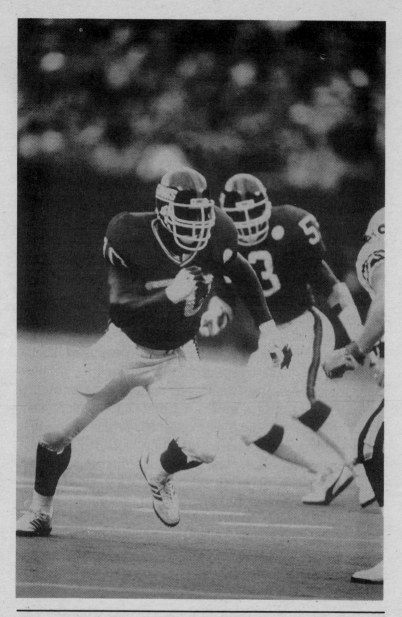

Hard to stop, Leonard Marshall played all out against Green Bay.
Focus on Sports

3 OFF AND RUNNING

It came as no surprise when Parcells announced that Simms would be his first string quarterback for the 1990 season. Nor was anyone particularly shocked when Leonard Marshall and Lawrence Taylor both signed their contracts in time for the first game against the Philadelphia Eagles.

But the display of football excellence that Taylor put on in that first game of the season was really a surprise—a pleasant one.

Taylor alone outplayed all eleven men on the Eagles' offense. He ran around them, over them and sometimes he just picked them up and threw them out of the way. Taylor also sacked Eagles' quarterback Randall Cunningham three times. That does not happen very often to Cunningham, who is one of the league's best scramblers.

On Philadelphia's third offensive play of the game, LT broke through the Philadelphia linesmen and charged like a mad bull at Cunningham. Being a sensible man, Randall jumped out of the way and threw the ball downfield to his tight end, Mickey Shuler. It looked like an excellent pass until Giants' defensive back Everson Walls intercepted and ran it in for a touchdown. The Giants had seven points and the game had barely begun.

While Cunningham and company put up a brave fight, the final score of 27–20 made it sound closer than it really was. The Giants' 1990 season started as well as anyone could have hoped.

There was more to it than just winning the first game. Aside from the Eagles, the Giants' only serious competition was the Washington Redskins. The Washington team was excellent, but unlucky against the Giants.

As for the other two teams in the division, there was little for the Giants to worry about. The Dallas Cowboys were rebuilding because many of their best players had retired. The Phoenix (formerly St. Louis) Cardinals had just lost their excellent quarterback, Neil Lomax, and were looking for a replacement. They asked the Giants about trading for Hostetler, but the answer was an extremely firm, "No."

After the difficult opening game against Philadelphia, the schedule favored the Giants. In the next three weeks, they played Dallas, Miami and Dallas, again. The Giants had the fifth week off. Since Dallas was no challenge, that left only Miami standing between the New Yorkers and a perfect start.

Miami proved not to be a problem either, as the Giants romped to a 20–3 victory. But one moment at the very end of that game caused sports fans all over New York to gasp in concern. Lawrence Taylor, playing his third straight game of high-powered football, suddenly pulled up lame on one of the final plays. He clutched his lower right leg in agony.

This came as a shock to many fans, because Taylor usually did not admit he was hurt even when he was seriously injured. He had once played three straight weeks with a small broken bone in his leg. But now he sat down on the field and called for the Giants' team paramedic, while the other players and their fans watched in deep concern. If Taylor was out for the season this would prove to be a costly win.

The good news was that Taylor had only a minor injury. The bad news was that it was the sort of minor injury that resulted from not being in good condition.

At home in Giants Stadium, Lawrence Taylor never let up against the Cowboys. *Focus on Sports*

Apparently, even a superstar like Lawrence Taylor should go through training camp each summer.

It turned out that it did not matter much as far as the Giants' season was concerned. Carl Banks was already a magnificent linebacker, almost as good as Taylor.

Taylor's mishap enabled Carl Banks and Pepper Johnson to emerge from the shadows proving their skills as linebackers. The fourth linebacker position was filled by Gary Reasons and Steve DeOssie, who each took the field on certain plays. On many NFL teams, a player like either Reasons or DeOssie would have been the best linebacker available.

As usual, the Giants also excelled at their punting game, with Sean Landeta kicking the ball harder and

Lawrence Taylor watched from the sidelines as the offense did its job. *Ron Vesely/Focus on Sports*

higher than many had dreamed was possible. One of the tricks of punting is to put the ball out of play near the other team's goal line. If it rolls into the end zone, that counts as a touchback and play starts at the 20-yard line. But if it goes out of bounds, or a player on the kicking team "downs" the ball before it reaches the end zone, the other team starts wherever the ball was downed.

A reserve cornerback named Reyna Thompson proved incredibly good at downing Landeta's punts in this manner. Thompson, whose first name is pronounced like "Renee," would speed down the field to where the ball was expected to land. With a wide, overhand swoop he would reach out and grab it, placing the football down in bounds, to the delight of Giants' fans and obvious annoyance of the other team.

During their week of rest, the Giants picked up another important player, placekicker Matt Bahr. The previous kicker, Raul Allegre, had developed frequent problems with pulled leg muscles. This happens to everyone who goes around kicking footballs 40 or 50 yards at a time. But Parcells was worried about Allegre's reliability, even though Allegre had done excellent work for the team.

Like most placekickers, Bahr was small and wiry, just slightly bigger than Dave Meggett. Hostetler, who served as holder on placekicks, had to spend a good amount of time working with Bahr, making sure they were familiar with each other's reflexes and reactions. Placekicking only looks easy.

In any case, Hoss was happy to feel useful, since he did not play much in those first four victories. Nor did he get to quarterback the team in Week Six, against the Redskins. This was a typical Giants–Redskins game, with the New Yorkers getting a lot of lucky breaks and

Washington's bespectacled Coach Joe Gibbs kicking the turf in frustration. The Redskins were an excellent football team, possibly as good as the Giants. But if anything could go wrong for them when playing Parcells' team, it did.

Two Giants excelled on offense early in the season. One was Simms, who played close to perfection as quarterback, giving up only two interceptions in the first ten games. He did this by hurling quick, low-risk passes to his receivers and handing off to his runners. The most notable of those runners was Ottis Anderson.

The former Cardinal was supposed to be too old for pro football, but no one had explained that to Anderson. He regularly plowed through opposing defenses, casually holding the ball in the crook of his right arm. That appearance was deceptive. Anderson's legs churned up the field as he searched for openings through which to run. He showed superb reflexes, often jumping sideways to avoid onrushing oversized tacklers. Even his short gains drew mad applause from Giants' faithfuls in the stadium.

Sportswriters soon noticed that Anderson was on the road to gaining 1,000 yards for the Giants this season. That is the benchmark for a terrific year at running back. Ottis had first done so as a Cardinal running back in 1979. He had again gained 1,000-plus yards several times in the 1980s. If he gained that many yards this year, it would make him the first player ever to have 1000-yard seasons in three different decades. That didn't happen, but in the course of the season Ottis did become the eighth man in NFL history to gain a total of more than 10,000 yards in his career.

Simms was injured during the sixth game, at home against Phoenix. When it happened, the Giants were

Here Simms was in excellent condition, ready to throw a pass.
Focus on Sports

already losing to the Cardinals. The New Yorkers had so underrated Phoenix they did not feel it was necessary to play very hard. When Hostetler came in to replace Simms, he did badly, too. Hoss had not played much since training camp and he was rusty. By the time he began throwing well, Phoenix had a nine-point lead with just a few minutes left in the game.

Hoss then took charge and led the Giants on a highly impressive pair of scoring drives. The first ended with a long touchdown pass to Stephen Baker, The Touchdown Maker. This was especially sweet for Hoss, who had scrambled on the play. If Simms had been in the game, he might have been sacked. When the New Yorkers got the football again, Hoss expertly led them down the field

It took three Redskins to pull down a sure-footed Anderson. *Focus on Sports*

and held the ball as Bahr kicked it through the uprights for three points. That was the last play of the game and it proved the Giants' wisdom in choosing Bahr over the other available kickers. Bahr had been around the league for ten years and had once kicked for the Pittsburgh Steelers as they won a Super Bowl. He was used to dealing with pressure—as he showed with this last-second field goal in the Cardinal game.

Coach Parcells was beaming as he ran happily across the field towards the Giants' clubhouse. When he realized that a TV camera was pointed at him, Parcells leaped in the air, smiled, waved his right fist in victory.

He continued to laugh through the next four weeks as the Giants barrelled over the Redskins, Colts, Rams and

Matt Bahr—at home in Giants Stadium—kicked another flawless field goal. *Focus on Sports.*

Pepper Johnson and LT tackled Redskin, Earnest Byner during the first quarter at RFK Stadium. *AP/Wide World Photos*

Lions. It seemed as though nobody was going to defeat the Giants this year. The next Redskins game centered on more lucky breaks. At one point a pass that should have gone for a Redskins' touchdown bounced off the receiver's shoulder pads and was intercepted by the Giants. Instead of kicking the turf, Redskins' Coach, Joe Gibbs kicked the bench in frustration.

That victory over Washington could be credited mainly to luck.

By Game Ten, against the Lions, the Giants' mastery of the opposition had reached the point where Parcells felt he could afford to be charitable. With his team ahead 20–0 at halftime, the Coach told his Giants to go easy in the second half, just use up the clock and get the game over as quickly as possible. There was nothing to be gained by scoring any more points and there was no joy to be had in humiliating another team.

The Giants went out and quickly disposed of Detroit in a scoreless second half.

Mark Bavaro crushed a Lion in a shut-out against Detroit.
AP/Wide World Photos

Parcells sent unmistakable signals from the sidelines. *Focus on Sports*

4 GREAT EXPECTATIONS

Parcells' act of charity was one of the last bright spots in the Giants' picture for some time. Their so-far perfect season fell apart with three losses in the next four weeks, which made people wonder if maybe those first ten wins hadn't been plain luck.

Trouble began in Philadelphia, when during Game 11 Eagles' quarterback, Randall Cunningham bounced back from early defeats and was tearing apart the league. The nimble Cunningham is a difficult man to defeat when things are going badly for him. When he's at his best and his teammates are playing well—watch out!

Part of the problem in Game 11 was that the Eagles *had* to win while the Giants just *wanted* to win. Another problem was that the Giants were looking ahead to their next game, against San Francisco, while the Eagles were concentrating on clobbering the Giants. Even when Pepper Johnson caused two fumbles in the first quarter and the Giants recovered both, it was still clear that Philadelphia was playing a stronger game.

Nor did it help much when, after the first fumble, Mark Ingram dropped a perfect pass from Simms on the Eagles' 5-yard line. Given the opportunity to recover from their early mistakes, the Eagles proceeded to make the Giants look foolish.

Having made the mistake in Philadelphia of looking ahead to the San Francisco game, the Giants then spent the next week looking back at the Eagles' game. It did not help matters that both games were played on the road. Everyone plays better at home when the stadium crowd is cheering rather than when 50,000-plus people are booing. Half the regular-season games are at home, but bad luck put the Giants on the road against two very good teams in a row. That meant two straight weeks of travel by airplane, staying in hotels in strange cities and worrying about losing too many more games.

At stake in San Francisco was the question of who would have the best National Conference record of the season. The teams with the two best records get to relax during the first week of playoffs, which is called "drawing a bye." Of those two best teams, the one with the better record gets to play its first post-season game with a home-field advantage.

Both the Giants and the San Francisco 49ers had records of 10–1. Both had excellent teams. But the 49ers are very hard to beat when they play at home.

To give the Giants credit, they put up a good fight in San Francisco. Even though they lost, 7–3, it was mostly due to a few lucky bounces that favored the 49ers. As sportswriters across America commented, it takes an excellent defense to limit San Francisco to just seven points in an entire game.

But those same writers pointed out that the Giants would need a stronger offense than the one that had just scored three points if they wanted to win another Super Bowl. Maybe, just maybe, they would have been better off with a scrambler like Hostetler as quarterback.

But Coach Parcells refused to even think about it. Simms had brought the team to a record of 10–2, which was second best in the entire league. He had played exceptionally well and thrown hardly any interceptions. By Parcell's standards, there was no way to justify putting Simms on the bench.

Other writers pointed out that the Giants' biggest gain had come on a play when Simms fumbled and Ottis Anderson picked up the ball and ran 20 yards with it.

32

Maybe, they joked, the Giants should fumble toward Anderson more often.

There was more laughter the following week as the Giants returned home to a convincing victory over Minnesota. Simms had one of his best games as he zipped one pass after another downfield. This was a Minnesota team that many thought would make the playoffs. The previous week, they had run all over the excellent Chicago Bears by a score of 41–13. But Simms made the Minnesotans look like amateurs. He stayed behind his blocking and made sure that the odds were in his favor

Simms handed off to the unstoppable Ottis Anderson. *Focus on Sports*

Mark Bavaro—as hard to handle as ever! *Focus on Sports*

on every pass. Simms threw a lot of short passes to his running backs and tight ends, then watched with pleasure as they charged downfield for big gains. He had gotten in the habit of celebrating each good play by leaping off the ground and zooming his right fist forward, like a boxer connecting with a punch. Phil was clearly enjoying himself.

After the Minnesota game, the nay-sayers were back to supporting Simms. Eleven wins in 13 weeks put the Giants exactly where they had been in their Super Bowl season four years earlier. Simms had been their quarterback then, too. He was now leading the league in every important statistic by which quarterbacks are judged. The most vital of these is the comparison of touchdown passes to interceptions given up. A good quarterback is somebody who throws at least as many TDs as interceptions. Simms, with 15 touchdown passes and only four interceptions, was having a wonderful year.

But the same was true of Jim Kelly, quarterback of the Buffalo Bills team that was the Giants' next opponent. The Giants had home field advantage, but the Bills had a surprise in store—one they had been working on all year. They called it the no-huddle offense.

Basically, the idea was that Buffalo planned each series of plays before they went on the field. So, instead of huddling after each play they would just go back and line up, then run their next play. If any changes had to be made in their planning, Kelly would let the others know this by way of a spoken code that he would yell out before the center hiked him the ball.

There was really nothing new in this. Every team in football uses a no-huddle offense if they get the ball at the end of the first or second half with little time left.

The no-huddle approach is rougher on the defense than the offense. Among other things, it leaves little time for reserves to run on the field. It also makes it difficult for the defense to figure out what the offense is planning.

When Buffalo Coach, Marv Levy decided to try the no-huddle approach full-time he trained his players to prepare for it. As a result, the Buffalo offense worked extremely hard in training camp. When they tried the no-huddle during regular season games, the other teams were "Buffaloed."

Levy planned to make the Giants' game the first in which his Bills would use the no-huddle for an entire four quarters. He expected the Giants' defense to be exhausted by half-time from trying to keep up with this game plan.

The Giants, of course, had no way of knowing what Levy was planning, but they did know that Buffalo was a superb football team. Even with the home field advantage at Giants Stadium, the Giants were in for a tough battle.

To make matters worse, a freezing rain fell on the ballpark that Sunday. It was difficult for Giants' fans to get there. When they did arrive, few felt like cheering. They mostly stood under umbrellas.

The players, of course, didn't have that option. They had to struggle along on the slick wet field between the goal posts. On days like that, the team with the best runners usually wins, because a lot of perfectly good passes get dropped.

As it happened, both teams had good runners. Buffalo's fullback Jamie Mueller was a powerful blocker, opening wide areas for running back Thurman Thomas to run through. Giants' blocking back Carthon did the same for Ottis Anderson. Both teams scored early. At the half, Buffalo led 14–10. But by that time both teams had lost their starting quarterbacks.

When Kelly injured his hand, it meant that Buffalo had to stop using the no-huddle, because the team was less familiar with backup QB Frank Reich. So the Giants' defense was able to play more effectively against a more normal offense.

The injury to Phil Simms meant that Jeff Hostetler

had to charge on the field and get the Giants moving. Hoss did not yet know that Simms' injury would keep that star quarterback out of all future Giants games in the 1990–91 season. All Hostetler knew was that his own chances of someday being a first string quarterback would be improved if he could turn things around and lead his team to victory over Buffalo.

It did not work out that way. Each team scored only one field goal in the entire second half as Buffalo won, 17–13. No one blamed Hoss. Even the best scrambling quarterback has trouble on a sopping wet field in nearly freezing weather. Buffalo won because their no-huddle offense scored more points than the Giants early in the game, before the wet field made it so difficult for anyone to stand up.

But the fact remained that Hostetler had not led the Giants to victory. Since many observers expected Buffalo to win the American Football Conference championship and go on to the Super Bowl, this looked bad for the Giants. If they could not beat Buffalo at Giants Stadium during the regular season, they might be unable to beat Buffalo at the Super Bowl.

Furthermore, the Giants had now lost three games out of four. The earlier 10-game winning streak was yesterday's news. The question was whether the Giants were exhausted: too spent to be anything more than half-decent in post-season.

More questions were asked during the remaining two weeks of the year, as Hostetler led the Giants to a pair of unimpressive victories over Phoenix and New England. In both cases, the Giants looked tired and Hostetler was forced to do a lot of desperate scrambling in order to win.

That was no disgrace against Phoenix, a team which had done a good job of rebuilding and played quite well during the season's second half. But the New England Patriots were generally regarded as the worst team in football. They were having a truly awful year until Game 16, when they nearly upset the Giants. Part of it was due to the fact that this game meant nothing to the Giants, while the Patriots had a chance to end their season on a big win. But, even so, the Patriots should not have given the Giants as much trouble as they did.

Coach Parcells later explained that he had ordered his men to run plays against New England that were tests for the playoffs. This sort of on-field rehearsal caused the Giants to make mistakes and miss opportunities. But fans and sportswriters did not know this at the time.

All that the New York football-watching community knew for a fact was that, except for the win over Minnesota, the last six weeks had been a real letdown. The experienced Phil Simms was finished for the year and the inexperienced Jeff Hostetler was in charge. Lawrence Taylor and Leonard Marshall had played sub-par most of the season. In the final weeks, Ottis Anderson had begun to show his age and gain far fewer yards.

Many sportscasters felt that the Giants had little chance of winning the Super Bowl. Sure, they would probably triumph over the Chicago Bears in the first week of the playoffs. But, after that, the Giants were probably in trouble.

Since many of the stars of their Super Bowl win four years earlier were getting too old for football, it looked like the Giants' glory was fading. Predictions for who would win the Super Bowl varied, but hardly anyone favored the Giants.

Except for Bill Parcells, who confidently said the Giants would win it all!

5 FIRST PLAYOFF

The Giants had won a week off in the first round of the playoffs. That was because they had the second-best record in the National Conference. The 49ers, who had the best record, also got to watch football that first playoff Sunday, instead of having to play the game.

The four National Conference teams to play in the first round were Chicago, New Orleans, Washington and Philadelphia. Many Giants' fans recalled their heroes' defeat by Philadelphia in Game 11 and hoped that the Redskins would defeat Philly before the Eagles got another shot at the Giants.

That's exactly what happened. The Redskins outplayed the Eagles, earning a second-week playoff game against San Francisco. Then the Bears polished off the New Orleans Saints, winning a trip to New York.

That first round "bye" made a big difference to the Giants, who were rested in preparation for the Bears game. The Giants had spent two weeks at home, practicing a lot but not playing football. The Bears, on the other hand, had spent a week in New Orleans, played a tough game against the Saints and then traveled to New York.

That proved to be just one of the big advantages the Giants had in this game. Their second edge was Jeff Hostetler—heroic scrambler—who was still replacing the injured Simms.

A sopping-wet second half against Buffalo and the two games which followed helped get Jeff into shape. Earlier in the year, when he came off the bench to help defeat Phoenix at Giants Stadium, Hoss had been rusty. He then returned to the bench for six weeks.

But now, in the important first playoff, he was more

than ready. This was the role Jeff had been preparing for all his life—championship quarterback.

Hoss ran six times against the Bears and gained 43 very important yards. The six Hostetler runs brought the New Yorkers five first downs and one touchdown. That was clearly the difference between winning and losing. Without those six big plays, the Giants might have spent a long afternoon watching Sean Landeta punt the football.

Looking back, it is hard to imagine Phil Simms having made those runs for first downs. That drop-back passer could easily have been tackled for losses on any or all of those plays. It is possible that Simms would have successfully run the football, too. But there is no question that Hoss runs better than Simms.

Sparked by Hoss' scrambling, the Giants won by the lopsided score of 31–3. This was a pleasant surprise to many of their fans. The team's assistant coach in charge of the offense, Ron Erhardt, later called it the Giants' best game of the season.

It was also the best game of Jeff Hostetler's career up to that point. Hoss had not just led the Giants to a big playoff victory, he had led them there by his own excellent playing. If the other Giants had any doubts about Hoss' ability before that Chicago game, those doubts were gone. As the Giants began practice for their next game against San Francisco, they watched the video-tapes of their victory over Chicago. They saw Hoss scramble away from one oversized Bear after another. But what they saw was not Hostetler running scared. They saw a confident, efficient Hostetler sprinting with the ball until he saw an open Giants' receiver downfield. Then, on the run, he would fire the ball to such favorite receivers as Mark Bavaro or Stephen Baker. It was a

Hoss called signals in post-season playoff action against the Bears. *Focus on Sports*

pleasant video for the Giants to watch.

The team divided its week of practice between New York and San Francisco. Coach Parcells believed in getting his men acclimated to the site of their most important road game. Getting used to the San Francisco climate proved easy. San Francisco has basically the same weather as New York, just slightly warmer.

In practice, Hoss worked with his receivers on the one key difference between his methods and those of Simms. With Simms in charge, the receiver's job is to run out the pass pattern that Simms assigns. With Hoss, the job is to run out that pattern and then see if Hoss is scrambling. If he scrambles, it is up to the receiver to get free and make sure Hoss sees him. If that means ignoring the planned pattern, then said pattern should be ignored.

Bavaro, in particular, had a gift for this type of broken-pattern play. The big tight end could usually sense where Hoss would want him to be on any given play. This was to prove vital in beating the 49ers.

Also vital was Hoss, the man throwing the ball to Bavaro. As Bears' coach Mike Ditka told reporters, "Hostetler is one of the best quarterbacks in the league."

41

Lawrence Taylor against the 49ers. *AP/Wide World Photos*

MEETING THE FEARSOME 49ERS

No one had beaten the 49ers in a playoff game for quite some time. The San Franciscoans had been easily the best pro football of the 1980s, winning the Super Bowls of 1981, 1984, 1988 and 1989. If the 49ers had beaten the Giants, they would have been the first team ever to win three consecutive Super Bowls.

The leader of the 49ers was Joe Montana, considered one of the best quarterbacks of *all time*, and a scrambler like Hoss. In his years on the Giants' bench, Hostetler always found hope in the fact that Montana, the league's winningest quarterback, was a scrambler. Most important Montana almost never fumbled and threw very few interceptions. The entire 49ers' offense was built around Montana, with good reason.

As he proved in the opening drive of this Conference championship game, Montana could also do many small things to perfection. On one key third down play he made a short little toss to receiver Mike Sherrard. This was not just a short pass by pro standards; it would have counted as a little toss in a schoolyard game. But Sherrard caught it for a five-yard gain and a first down.

One play like that after another moved the 49ers to the Giants' 20-yard line. There, they attempted a field goal. Since the goal posts are ten yards back in the end zone and the kicker stands seven yards behind scrimmage, that means a 37-yard kick. The kick was good. The 49ers now led by 3–0.

One good drive deserves another, as Hoss demonstrated. He expertly drove the Giants up the field toward the goal line. A key play was an eight-yard run for a first down by Ottis Anderson, that wonderful warhorse. Ottis

43

then added an 11-yard gain. But Hoss was the main engine of that drive. He fired one 20-yard pass to Mark Ingram for a first down. Another first down came on a pass interference penalty against San Francisco. Then Hoss held the ball in place as Matt Bahr booted it in from 28 yards out. The game was one-fifth over and the score was tied.

The Giants stopped the Montana men, forcing a punt. As the game progressed, it became obvious that Lawrence Taylor had regained his old form. After a season in which it seemed that the magic was waning from Taylor's linebacking, he was proving a powerful onfield force.

Hoss then drove the Giants to a 6–3 lead as Bahr kicked another field goal. This time, the most important play was Hoss' four-yard run for a first down. That was one yard more than he needed. The Hostetler running style is something like that of a greyhound dog at full sprint. Hoss' whole body goes into the effort, which in this case ended in a great hooking slide.

Bahr's highly impressive 42-yard kick was matched a few moments later by San Francisco kicker Mike Cofer, who toed the ball in from 35 yards out. The score was now 6–6 and it remained knotted for the rest of the half. Once again, the powerful 49ers were crashing against the equally-powerful Giants. At any second, fans expected to see sparks fly. These were two magnificent football teams, each playing the game almost to perfection.

The Giants were down by four points and time was running out. They needed two field goals to win, provided they kept San Francisco from scoring again. The first of those needed field goals came from a trick play that Parcells had set up before game time.

Hostetler proved his ability once again against four-time Super Bowl champions San Francisco. *Thearon Henderson/Focus on Sports*

Bill Parcells cheered his superstars to victory over San Francisco for the chance to play in Tampa. *Thearon Henderson/Focus on Sports*

When the Giants punted, linebacker Gary Reasons lined up in front of punter Sean Landeta. Reasons would then call the signals and block for Landeta. But, according to the rules, there was nothing to stop the center from hiking the football to Reasons, instead of Landeta. Parcells had told Reasons that, if the 49ers provided him with the right opportunity, he should call for a fake punt and run with the ball.

That happened in the fourth quarter. The 49ers, afraid that Landeta and Reyna Thompson would down the football near their goal line, forgot about Reasons. Seeing a tremendous gap in the middle of the 49er defense, Reasons called for the football. He ran 30 yards with it before the shocked and angry 49ers brought him down. When Bahr kicked a field goal soon afterwards, the Giants trailed by 13–12.

That might have been the end of the scoring on that bright, sunny day in San Francisco. But the Giants refused to be defeated. San Francisco got the football and tried to put together a long, time-consuming drive that would end the game. All the 49ers had to do was keep getting first downs until the clock ran out. They did not need to score again.

Every Giants' defender made a brave effort to stop the drive—especially LT

Giants' defensive linesman Erik Howard can be a powerful force, too. With 2:36 left in the game, 49er running back, Roger Craig took the football and ran with it. Howard's helmet bashed the ball from Craig's hands. Taylor fell on the football.

The stage was now set for high drama, with Jeff Hostetler in the leading role. Somehow, he had to drive his team 30 yards against one of the finest defenses in the history of pro football. Then he had to hope that Matt Bahr would be able to kick yet another field goal.

Nineteen of those 30 yards came on a scrambling pass to Bavaro.

"That was supposed to be a dropback pass," Hoss later told reporters, "but, when the pass rush got heavy, I moved out to the right."

Downfield, Bavaro saw Hoss scramble, so he threw out the pass pattern. His one goal was to get open enough for Hoss to throw him the ball. Hoss threw. Mark caught. Several large 49ers belted Bavaro, trying to get him to drop the ball, but Bavaro held on for the big gain.

One more decent pass play would put the New Yorkers within Bahr's field goal range. But the game clock was running down.

Hoss called for a "bootleg," a play in which the quarterback runs toward the sideline and throws the football to a waiting receiver. Stephen Baker made the catch.

"Baker did a good job of coming back to the ball at the sidelines," Hoss later said, "and he stepped out of bounds to stop the clock."

So Matt Bahr went into his specialty act one more time. Four field goals in one game was already an impressive total. But Bahr knew that his work this day would be remembered for his fifth effort. If it was good, Bahr would be the hero. Otherwise, he would be the goat.

On the sidelines, eight Giants got on their knees and held hands. Some were praying. Others were just silently watching the field.

Hostetler called for the ball, which was perfectly snapped to him. He placed it on the ground in front of Bahr. The kicker's toe punched into the football and it flew toward the goal posts. Seventy thousand football fans stood in silence as the ball rose, straight and true.

48

Leonard Marshall brought the 49ers to their knees.
Focus on Sports

Then there was a loud sigh of disappointment from the
49ers' fans as the referee signalled that Bahr had scored
again.

The Giants seized each other in delight, cheering
happily. Hoss, who had the best view, leaped in the air
and rocketed his fist skyward. Then he shook hands with
the extremely happy Matt Bahr.

The Giants were going to the Super Bowl!

Matt Bahr's years of hard training paid off for the Giants as he helped lead them to victory in Super Bowl XXV. *Focus on Sports*

7 BATTLE WITH THE BUFFALO BILLS

With each passing week the Giants were showing more faith in Hostetler. In turn, he was growing more confident in himself.

While the team flew down to Tampa for the Super Bowl against the Buffalo Bills, Parcells and his staff worked out a plan for beating the no-huddle offense. The plan was simple: Don't give them the ball.

Like all bright ideas, this was easier said than done, but there was no arguing with the logic. If the Giants put together long, time-consuming drives that ended in touchdowns and field goals, the impact of Buffalo's no-huddle would be limited. Buffalo would have less chance to score and the Giants' defense would be less exhausted.

As Hoss dressed for the game, he knew that the greatest pressure would be on him. On the one hand, this made it clearer than ever that his coaches considered Hoss an excellent quarterback. On the other hand, he knew that the Bills' pass rush would be ferocious.

His whole career was riding on the outcome of one game. Plus, that game was going to be broadcast to a worldwide audience. There were 78,000 people in the stands at Tampa Stadium. But tens of millions of people would be viewing by television in the United States and Canada. Millions more would be watching around the world, especially in Western Europe, where American football was gaining in popularity. There would be fans listening via short-wave radio from as far away as the Australian Outback and the mountains of Northern India. There would also be an important audience of Americans serving in the Persian Gulf. A big halftime

51

show was planned to honor America's men and women fighting there.

At first, all went well for the Giants. They got the ball and Hoss went to work. He relied on Ottis Anderson and Dave Meggett, the oldest and youngest men on his squad. Repeatedly, the powerful Anderson crashed into the Buffalo line, clawing for an extra few inches as the Bills dragged him down. The short, speedy Meggett charged through gaps in Buffalo's wall of flesh. As always, it was hard to find Meggett in a crowd.

The drive petered out at Buffalo's 28-yard line. Matt Bahr strode onto the field and waited for his teammates to line up. He then confidently booted the football between the uprights for a three-point lead.

Hostetler leaped into the air when he saw that the kick was good. He now knew that the Bills *could* be beaten, that the Giants *might* win.

But the rest of the first quarter and much of the second belonged to the Bills. Kelly directed his offense carefully. Despite excellent play by the Giants' defense, that first Bills' drive ended in a Scott Norwood field goal.

Hoss had difficulties. The Bills were angry and desperately wanted to win. The Giants' running plays were stopped. Passes were batted down. Then defensive end Leon Seals bashed into Hoss so hard that the Giants quarterback was almost left unconscious. Ottis Anderson helped Hoss to the sidelines, where the team doctor gave him an ammonia cap to sniff. It took a few minutes before Hoss could see straight again.

During those minutes, Kelly took charge of the game and the Bills' offense kept the Giants off-balance. Buffalo's heroes ran, then passed, then ran again. Kelly fired a long, high pass to Bills receiver James Lofton. The

52

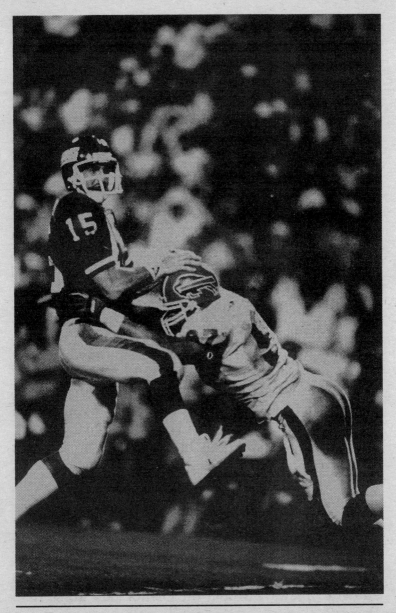

Hostetler threw the ball just in time during some heart-stopping action of Super Bowl XXV. *Focus on Sports*

Giants' Perry Williams thought he could intercept. But the ball bounced off Williams' hands and flew to Lofton. Buffalo gained 61 yards on that play. Lawrence Taylor, who had almost sacked Kelly, punched the ground in disappointment. Soon after, Don Smith of Buffalo ran the football into the end zone. It was now 10–3 Buffalo.

The Giants' game plan had been based on getting ahead in the scoring and then using up as much time as possible in order to keep Kelly and company off the field. Now, Hoss would have to concentrate as much on moving the team as on using up the clock. Even worse, Norwood's kickoff left the Giants deep in their own territory.

Hoss faded back into his own end zone, hoping to complete a long pass. As he faded back, Ottis Anderson stepped forward to block for him. Hoss tripped over Ottis. While Hoss was trying to regain his balance, defensive end, Bruce Smith knocked Hoss down in the end zone. Buffalo now led by 12–3!

Actually, it was at this embarrassing moment that the Giants and Hoss began to turn the game around. If Hoss had fumbled the football, Smith or another Buffalo player would have fallen on it. That would have meant a touchdown and a Buffalo lead of 17–3 instead of 12–3. But none of the Giants thought of that at the time. A 12–3 lead for a team like the Bills seemed tremendous.

As Smith and his buddies danced happily around the end zone, Hoss walked quietly off the field. In the broadcast booth, record books were checked to see what the worst defeat had ever been in a Super Bowl. It turned out to have been the previous year, when San Francisco beat Denver by a score of 55–10. Would this be a second straight runaway? Would the Giants look worse than Denver?

A lesser team would have conceded defeat. But, by

Ottis Anderson made a touchdown run during the third quarter of the Super Bowl to put the Giants ahead. *A/P/Wide World Photos*

sheer force of will, the Giants turned the game around. After the safety they were required to punt the ball to the Bills. Sean Landeta launched the ball mightily and the Giants roared downfield to tackle the Bill who caught it. They stopped Kelly and his offense from moving the ball. Buffalo's Rick Tuten punted to Meggett, who fought his way upfield as if his life depended on it.

Hoss began mixing his plays like an expert. Ottis Anderson ran repeatedly into the line. Sometimes, Ottis had the ball. Other times, he faked the run as Hoss rolled out and threw the football. Mark Bavaro made a sensational catch and ran downfield carrying several Bills. Dave Meggett found ways of getting open that no one had seen before.

55

Ottis Anderson charged the line yet again. *Focus on Sports*

The original game plan was scrapped, at least for this drive. With the Giants down 12–3, the only thing they cared about was getting back seven of those points. They could worry about the clock later. Right now, a touchdown was all that mattered—it would turn this game around.

Then The Touchdown Maker, Stephen Baker, broke free in the end zone. The ball zoomed out of Hoss' hand. It was still gaining speed when Baker grabbed it. He held on. The referee signalled "Score!" The crowd roared.

Hoss bounded through unhappy defenders to shake hands with Baker, who was being congratulated by every Giants' player within reach. The game was beginning to turn their way and they knew it. Bahr's extra point made the score 12–10 as the Giants ran off the field at halftime.

8 WINNING BY A FOOT

After the halftime break, the Giants charged out on the field quivering with excitement. When they got the ball again you could see that these guys were hungry for glory. Even though they had already played two exhausting quarters of pro football, nobody was admitting he was tired.

Unlike their final drive of the first half, the Giants began playing more cautious football. They knew that a fumble or interception could hurt them badly. Hoss made good use of Ottis Anderson, a man who almost never fumbles. That day, Ottis was at his best. He was proving he was not too old for football. In fact, he was proving that he was still a terrific running back. Time and again, the Giants' line burst through the defense to clear a path for Ottis. Blocking back Maurice Carthon charged ahead of Ottis like a bulldozer, knocking down everyone in his path. The Bills tried to force Ottis to fumble each time. But he sensed that victory was in his grasp.

Hoss also made very good use of his receivers, especially the tight ends. Bavaro, always at his best under pressure, moved through the Bills like a Sherman tank. Howard Cross, usually thought of as merely a blocker, proved that he had good hands. Buffalo put up a fight but the Giants kept advancing.

It ended with Anderson bulling into the end zone from the one-yard line. That was the second Super Bowl touchdown of Ottis' career. The first had been four years earlier, when many people thought he was playing his final game as a pro.

Bahr's extra point made it 17–12 Giants. Even the

Bills' fans were cheering. No matter who you were rooting for, it was one fantastic game of football!

Even though the Giants had now scored the last 14 points, the game was a long way from finished. They only led by five and either a pair of Buffalo field goals or a Buffalo touchdown would put the Bills back in front. Momentum has a way of changing sides.

Buffalo's powerful offense went into overdrive. Without hurdles, and with a lot of self-confidence of their own, Kelly's Heroes charged down the field. The Giants' superb defense looked dazed. Kelly kept them that way with one power play after another.

It led to a 31-yard dash by Thurman Thomas, the Bills' great runner. He bounced off several Giants tacklers. It was like trying to stop a truck. Thomas barrelled into the end zone with his hands held high, celebrating his own touchdown. When Norwood kicked the extra point, Buffalo led by 19–17. There was more than 14 minutes left in the game and, suddenly, it looked like Buffalo might win.

The Giants' offense refused to consider that possibility. They got the ball back on their 23-yard line and pounded their way ahead, slowly capturing ground from the bone-tired Bills.

"You could see them sagging, tiring out," Carthon later told a reporter. "Our left side was really coming off the ball—right at Bruce Smith—and any time you see a great player like Smith just barely getting down in his stance, you *know* he's tired."

But the Giants were also worn out and had to depend yet again on Matt Bahr. He kicked his second three-pointer of the day and put the Giants up by 20–19.

Their drive followed the original Giants' game plan of using up as much time as possible. In fact, the 13-plays

58

Lawrence Taylor, Bill Parcells and Carl Banks celebrated as champions, seconds after Norwood's failed field goal attempt.
Focus on Sports

had used up more than seven minutes off the game clock. This meant that the Bills, even though they only needed one field goal to get back in front, were running short of time.

Rick Tuten punted to the Giants. The Buffalo defense held firm. Sean Landeta boomed another punt down toward the Buffalo end of the stadium. There was 2:16 left on the clock and the Bills were on their own 10-yard line.

Field goals have been kicked from as far as 53 yards away. But that does not happen very often. Even for a good kicker like Norwood, the line of scrimmage usually has to be inside the other team's 30. That meant Kelly had to move the Bills 60 yards in a short period of time.

Somehow, Kelly got them there. As Giants' fans around the globe moaned, the no-huddle offense worked one last time for that season. With time left for just one play, the Bills stood on the Giants' 29-yard line. It was all up to Scott Norwood.

59

Norwood was facing the same challenge that Bahr had dealt with the previous week in San Francisco. Again, there were players on both teams kneeling in prayer.

The ball was snapped and held in place for Norwood. His kicks tend to hook left, so he aimed slightly to the right. Marshall, Taylor and nine other Giants struggled to block the kick. But nobody came close.

Mark Bavaro, one of the best tight ends of all time, proved it in the Super Bowl. *Focus on Sports*

Ottis Anderson "flew" toward becoming Super Bowl MVP.
A/P/Wide World Photos

The ball rose off the ground. Everyone on the field watched to see if it would hook through the uprights. But Norwood could see that he had missed and walked sadly from the field.

Jeff Hostetler continued to watch as the ball sailed wide to the right. In that final moment Hoss had achieved tremendous success. He was now one of just 15 players ever to quarterback a team to victory in the 25-year history of the Super Bowl.

On the field, Coach Parcells gleefully hugged the two Giants nearest him, who happened to be Lawrence Taylor and Carl Banks.

Assorted Giants and their coaches were pounding each other in delight. Hardly anyone had expected the

Lawrence Taylor gave Bills' Jim Kelly a run for his money. *Focus on Sports*

Giants to win Super Bowl XXV. They had won mainly because of their combined effort to achieve a victory.

Throughout the stadium, football fans remained on their feet, screaming with delight in honor of the Giants' achievement.

EPILOGUE

But, back in the Giants' locker room, Hoss was thinking of the season that had just ended. In five weeks he had led the Giants to five straight victories in the games he started. The applause and shouting continued and Hoss was placed front stage center, at last. There was no escaping the onslaught of congrats as reporters, team-mates and coaches alike swarmed the scene to mark this memorable moment in the history of sports.

That day, the Giants became the only team to employ two Super Bowl-winning quarterbacks. Even at that moment, questions were being asked about whether Simms or Hostetler would be the team's starter next year.

In the meantime, both Hoss and Simms could be extremely happy, since each had been instrumental—although at different times, in different seasons—in making their team Super Bowl champs. Ironically, these two gridiron gladiators shared the same experience from different vantage points: one rising to meet the moment, the other knowing how brief and fleeting a feeling it is to be a football hero.

VICTORY!